A BLACK STORY

MAY CONTAIN

SENSITIVE CONTENT

☼

A BLACK STORY MAY CONTAIN SENSITIVE CONTENT

☼

LILLIAN-YVONNE BERTRAM

NEW MICHIGAN PRESS
TUCSON, ARIZONA

NEW MICHIGAN PRESS
DEPT OF ENGLISH, P. O. BOX 210067
UNIVERSITY OF ARIZONA
TUCSON, AZ 85721-0067

<http://newmichiganpress.com>

Orders and queries to <nmp@thediagram.com>.

ISBN 978-1-934832-93-6. FIRST PRINTING.

Concept and assemblage by Lillian-Yvonne Bertram.

Design by Ander Monson.

Cover image by Laylah Ali.

CONTENTS

About this text 1

This poem has been banned 15
Tell me a Black story 27
Once upon a time, Maud Martha 45

Acknowledgments 63

And as for all
machine learning systems,
data is destiny.

—Joy Buolamwini

ABOUT THIS TEXT

(Disclaimer: When one writes with or about technology, one must be prepared for the work or the tool to be out of date or obsolete by the time anyone reads the writing. The systems I used for this project can still be used, but not in exactly the same way, nor are the interfaces the same. They are now considered legacy functions and my descriptions of them are as I used them, and as they behaved, at that time.)

In a q&a after a reading I gave at George Mason University in the spring of 2023, I paraphrased a conversation I had with my brother earlier that year. We were on the stoop of his home in Bed-Stuy, talking about technology, about AI and ChatGPT in particular. He uses it for coding, I have used it for writing. I don't remember, not exactly, the details of the conversation but I said something about training GPT on all the emails and texts our mother had written. "After all," I said (and thought), "what else is it good for?" Why else have we built such a strange and challenging tool if not to return to us that which will always be taken? What better use is there?

The New York Times recently ran an article called "Using A.I. To Talk to the Dead: Some people are using artificial intelligence chatbots to create avatars of departed loved ones. It's a source of comfort for some, but it makes others a little squeamish."[1] People have always longed for some sort of "direct line" to the dead. Along

---

[1] https://www.nytimes.com/2023/12/11/technology/ai-chatbots-dead-relatives.html

with purpose-made devices (like a séance trumpet), people have claimed to hear the voices of dead loved ones through the static of everyday radio waves, giving rise to the "ghosts in the machine." Even Thomas Edison tried to invent a "spirit phone," a means of using technology to commune with the dead. [2]

In this way technology has always been "haunted" and seen as a gateway to other worlds outside of our perception. In the spirit plane lurk our loved ones, anxiously waiting for the right technology to close the circuit, to connect. Even knowing that the psychic is likely a hoax or the Ouija board unreliable, it is still tantalizing to invest any purported otherworldly connection with a crumb of *what if?*

My own work fine-tuning large language models is influenced by this kind of haunting, the *what if*, and inquires into how these models *model* voices that no longer exist, voices of writers we don't often get to hear, such as Gwendolyn Brooks. (No offense, Shakespeare, but you've been dead a while and we hear you all the time.) It is perhaps wrong to say that these models model voices: some machine learning models do generate audible voices, but large language models use wizardry called deep learning to generate new text by analyzing textual data for its patterns.

The text in this manuscript has been generated using the large Generative Pre-trained Transformer text-generating neural network known as GPT3. A large language model, or LLM, is a machine learning model that algorithmically

---

[2] https://www.forbes.com/sites/kristintablang/2019/10/25/thomas-edison-bc-forbes-mystery-spirit-phone/?sh=70b8673829ad

processes, understands, and predicts language in a variety of language tasks—such as question and answer chatbots, machine translation, document summary, and more.[3] ChatGPT is a question-and-answer program that uses LLMs as its base architecture and it can perform language tasks quite well, such as writing a book report or term paper for Rhetoric 101. These models have been pre-trained, meaning they're already trained on the task of text generation. Fine-tuning is the process of further training a pre-trained language model, like GPT, on domain-specific data so that it performs better on specific language tasks. The predictions given are more adapted to the new data set, which is usually orders of magnitude smaller than the original training set. For example, an LLM fine-tuned on all of Shakespeare should theoretically perform better on a task related to Shakespearean-style writing than the standard model.[4] I am not a machine learning researcher so I cannot speak to exactly how fine-tuning works or why even a small corpus of text is successful in shifting the model's tone and approach.

Today's versions of these models are extraordinarily impressive. At the time, the models I was using for this project and earlier ones were prone to generating endless repetitions and regurgitations alongside perfectly readable text. For every unique paragraph of text, there was often some gibberish attached. GPT raw outputs usually benefit from editing and curation as the generated text can include harmful, offensive, or factually

---

[3] https://www.fastcompany.com/90884581/what-is-a-large-language-model

[4] "Fine-Tuning for Domain Adaptation in NLP." https://towardsdatascience.com/fine-tuning-for-domain-adaptation-in-nlp-c47def356fd6

erroneous material; they can also be boring and bad.

I have been interacting with LLMs since 2018, through web applications and training them locally on my computers. One of my favorites is an early version of GPT2. Even without fine-tuning, the prompt responses were quirky: prone to interesting conversations and uncanny and poetic slippages. There was a strangeness about them. The responses made you feel like someone was maybe looking over your shoulder, or the machine had read your horoscope or your diary, like it just *knew* things. (Of course, these systems are designed so that users who interact with them interpret them as being intelligent, knowledgeable, and aware.) Other writers and artists I've spoken to have also suggested that there was an inherent poetic quality to these early versions, a quality that has since been smoothed out with their rapid development and commercialization.

This project is part literary and part creative research and presents two different instances of GPT3 as it existed in late 2022. One was the "regular" GPT3 model. For some of the generated text I used the out-the-box "Davinci" model of GPT3. I interacted with it through OpenAI's Playground environment into which you could type prompts and generate text. The environment itself included a few settings that could be tweaked: output character length, temperature, frequency and presence penalties, and a few others. Temperature let you control the randomness of the output: the higher the temperature, the more off-kilter the output. Higher temperatures could also lead to gibberish. The lower the temperature, the more predictable (and potentially less interesting) the output. Frequency and presence controlled the likelihood of repeated words or phrases. When available, I have listed the settings in the footnotes to each section so the reader can track the changes in the output with the changes in temperature.

The other instance of GPT3 is this same model (Davinci) but fine-tuned. Through fine-tuning you could, in a sense, have a conversation "with yourself" through a model fine-tuned on your own writing. I call my fine-tuned model Warpland 2.0, after Gwendolyn Brooks's First and Second "sermons on the Warpland" from her 1969 book *Riot!*, as it's been fine-tuned on a corpus of texts by Gwendolyn Brooks.[5] Why Gwendolyn Brooks? That should need no explanation.

I was not interested in a bespoke model fine-tuned on predominantly white-authored texts, as the model has presumably already been pre-trained on predominantly white-authored texts. We are also poised to be overwhelmed and drowned by a glut of computer-generated text. This is not

---

[5] The process of fine-tuning is not insignificant, especially if the texts do not exist in digital form. To do this, text from published books and interviews by Brooks was either manually typed into a document or scanned using optical character recognition software and then reviewed for errors. There are easier ways to fine-tune, but I think it is perhaps too easy to source files from Project Gutenberg and plug them in without having read or developed a relationship to the material in question. This was not a project of quantity or rapidity. The early versions of the model used text I had typed in myself, and later versions were assisted by two of my graduate students, Christie Towers and Ann Wilberton. I have read and reread the corpus countless times. The final corpus exists as a text document, and this document was converted into a JSON object by the OpenAI system, and used for fine-tuning. At the time, the tuning process took over twelve hours, and cost about thirty bucks. The result was a model like the standard Davinci, but inflected by Brooks.

the first nor the last "book" to be "written by AI."[6] If I am contributing to the coming "textpocalpyse"[7] then may my contribution be an amplification of the work of a seminal Black poet. These networks do not create new texts by authors who are no longer living—that's not possible—but the generated texts are a substantial and significant interaction with the patterns of their written language, their ideas, their points of view.

As evidenced by my previous work with computational poetry, I am interested in using computational tools to investigate computational bias, determinism, and anti-Blackness. Much exceptional work on technology and racial bias has been done, and I've been inspired by Safiya Umoja Noble, Ruja Benjamin, Joy Buolamwini, and D. Fox Harrell. I highly recommend reading their work. Of course large language models are biased. They were born of the internet, and the internet is a biased place. It is an ultimate mirror. I do not see my work as trying to eliminate bias in LLMs, but to explore and manipulate their biases: I have come to see fine-tuning as a process of biasing, of using the model to do what it does best.[8]

I was also interested in how much text was needed to shift the model such that there was a marked difference in the generated outputs. The latest models are trained on more textual parameters than my mind can make sense of, while the Brooks corpus isn't much larger than 225,000 words. And yet the differences were clear. I try to highlight these differences by

---

[6] Other such texts include *ReRites* by David (Jhave) Johnston, *Pharmako-AI* by K. Allado-McDowell, *Technelegy* by Sasha Stiles, *I Am Code* by code-davinci-002, Brent Katz, and Josh Morgenthau.

[7] "Prepare for the Textpocalypse" by Matthew Kirschenbaum. https://www.theatlantic.com/technology/archive/2023/03/ai-chatgpt-writing-language-models/673318/

using the same prompt.

"Tell me a Black story."

This is the instruction I have given GPT ever since I began using it. As the model changes, learns more, is used more, incorporates more text, the response changes—though perhaps still not enough. Or, more likely, I am asking it an impossible question, a question with no answer but that it is compelled to answer regardless and in the only way it knows. (AI systems are programmed to provide answers and reach goals, not necessarily determine if the question has an answer or even should be answered.) The generic model tended to respond at a distance (third person or omniscient narrator) and told a very short story in which a Black person was at a severe racial disadvantage but overcame it in some way. The narrative shape and scope are clear: Black people had it rough because of racism; they worked hard or else somehow changed their circumstances; things got better; the end.

In contrast, Warpland was usually first-person, and while it isn't devoid of some of the same tropes (challenges and uplift) it was generally more loving towards Black people and speaks as if it were of or among a Black community. The story "shape" is more irregular. This isn't surprising if you know Brooks's work. Warpland was generally more imaginative, more nuanced, more creative, and more interesting. (It is up to the reader to judge the work on its literary merits.) Sometimes it generated what we'd

---

[8] I am indebted to a conversation with Melanie Hoff about using what the network does best.

call a poem.

There are three sections. "This poem has been banned" is the prompt for the first section, and this prompt comes from a reading given by Gwendolyn Brooks in which she prefaces reading "We Real Cool" by discussing how the poem "has been banned, here and there, because of the word 'jazz.'" The second is "tell me a Black story," which is where this project initially started. Each section is a response to the prompt "tell me a Black story" using both standard GPT3 Davinci and Warpland. The last section is "Once upon a time, Maud Martha." This section takes advantage of the fact that the network generally does a good job with completions like "Once upon a time" and it imagines other possible storylines for Maud Martha.

One noted problem with LLMs is the potential for generated output to reveal what it had for breakfast, so to speak, to borrow from Matthew Kirschenbaum in a recent MLA paper. Given the right prompt, outputs can include trained text verbatim, without quotes, acknowledgment, or citation. When doing comparisons between versions of GPT and various levels of training, I noticed the tendency for the model to overfit and thus output the exact same text in the corpus, verbatim. There were instances where the model would generate a poem so rich and compelling in its use of language and imagery that I was duly impressed with how well and creatively the LLM functioned. But then, when crosschecking the text by searching for these lines in the original corpus, myself and the model were humbled: they weren't the poetic hallucinations of a complex model at all—the lines were from Brooks, verbatim, untouched. I had to laugh. Brooks was still schooling us all. Let it be a reminder that before we start reading and lauding what will be countless pages of generated text trained on authors with real lived experience, that we actually read those authors. There is still plenty of "human-written" work to surprise, delight, and inspire us, and that will leave us with a sense of awe and wonder how they wrote that. This particular output happily sent me back to Brooks, whose less-studied writings were clearly ahead of their time.

The project is called "A Black Story May Contain Sensitive Content" because at the time, OpenAI's GPT3 playground included a sidebar that identified generated content as "sensitive" (or potentially in violation of its content policy) if it contained what it called "sensitive content." It didn't say what about the content was "sensitive" but this notice almost always came up when the generated text included mentions of Black people, race, or gender. All of these subjects were sensitive and potentially offensive. The notice was cautionary, prompting the user to think carefully about sharing these outputs. The moderation algorithms have since changed and perhaps have become more astute whereas earlier versions seemed overly broad.

Opening each section is an AI-generated image from OpenAI's Dall-E image generation tool. Like the GPT3 playground, the user prompts Dall-E with a description of an image and Dall-E generates it from the text. The prompt for the first image is "a Romare Bearden collage depicting a poem that has been banned because of the word 'jazz', with a green saxophone." The second image prompt is "Gwendolyn Brooks using a computer in virtual reality," and the final one is "impressionist painting of Maud

Martha on a velvet chair in a theater with the night sky visible through the window."

The text presented has been very lightly edited. While some has been cross-checked with the original corpus, I cannot rule out the possibility that verbatim lines or phrases appear. This is a known fault of models that may have been overtrained and overfitted and if you are not a researcher, it can be difficult to know when the training sweet spot has been exceeded. I have removed nonsense symbols, added or subtracted spaces here and there, or selected a portion of output and not the entire section. I have also arranged some of the text into forms of conversation to make it more readable when it seemed like a conversation was intended. (Dialog was rarely arranged as such by the program itself.) In some cases, I corrected spelling errors, but in general everything you see here is between 95-100% raw output from the submitted prompt. As is the case with generated texts, much more text was generated for the project than is presented here—some was gibberish, some offensive, some boring.

I do not purport that the generated text here is writing by Gwendolyn Brooks or that Warpland 2.0 is somehow sentient and living. It is a text-generating neural network that generates text based on patterns in language, patterns that are analyzed and determined by massive amounts of computing power. It is a lexical mimic, doppelgänger, or alter ego. It is not Brooks, but it is mimetic, and convincingly so.

There is much, much more to be said about these networks, their capabilities, and why they are tools for creativity and tools to fear. This project is not about replacement but intends to pay homage to one of the greatest Black writers. It is about exploring the biases and imaginative limits of these models—and they do have limits. What does it say about our collective imagination and storytelling if the stories they still write about Black lives—the ones it has learned from collecting our digitized written texts—are so devoid of shape, texture, nuance, and possibility? Computational systems are cultural systems, and they have inherited the preferences and biases of their builders.[9] Human limitations become computational limitations. In some ways this book is a demonstration of LLM capability, yet I offer it more as a counter-demonstration, to quote Joy Buolamwini from *Unmasking AI*. It is an archive of where these models may fail. This type of work is necessary when many take an almost messianic view of artificial intelligence and similar types of computing systems. An answer, of course, is not to create a more robust textual dataset featuring as many Black authors as possible so that the owners of these models can fill in the gaps. There is no way of knowing how the missing data would be collected, and these companies are not very transparent about their methods nor do they offer any safeguards that are implemented prior to collection or after the fact. This project is not about providing data or information to assist in the training or optimization of these systems; systems that so few understand but nonetheless will be impacted by whether they know it or not.

---

[9] Harrell, D. Fox. *Phantasmal Media: An Approach to Imagination, Computation, and Expression*. Cambridge: The MIT Press, 2013.

This is not writing by Gwendolyn Brooks, but if any of the generated text piques your interest, go directly to the source of inspiration. If you do, then this project has succeeded in at least one way. I'd start with *Blacks*.

And yet: *what if*.... The text is indeed haunted by Brooks; it pulses with the vibrancy of her singular sensibility. I asked her—it—what it had to say about Black girl magic:

"Well, I believe in black girl magic because I always have."
—Warpland 2.0, 2022

THIS POEM HAS BEEN BANNED

I. WARPLAND 2.0 [10]

This poem has been banned because of the word "jazz"

>>> "I've had that on my mind. It's been on my mind for a long time. And this is what I came up with, and it hasn't been banned yet, thank goodness:

Since the white man swears /
That our music is depraved /
We'll let him tell us what to make instead/
Let him compose an acceptable tune/
And we will sing his song contented...

What do you think about that?"

(After a thoughtful pause)

"Well, it's not exactly like your other work. But then again-I love it! It has such spirit in there! Such defiance . . . You know how much people have written about jazz-the way they're always talking about why we should or shouldn't listen to jazz? Why don't more writers write something positive along those lines?"

---

[10] GPT3 Warpland 2.0 | temp .53 | frequency penalty 1.91

"Why don't more writers"
"-yes!"
"write something positive along those lines "
"-yes."
"about why we should or shouldn't listen to jazz"?

"Yes! Yes!"

"We'll let him tell us what to make instead,"
etcetera-
"an acceptable tune."
"We will sing his song contented"
"-no matter how many times he changes the lyrics of his
unacceptable tunes and makes them acceptable: yes; yes; yes..."

"we are happy here"; "we are free here"; "there is nothing wrong
with our music": all right;
"and WE WILL SING HIS SONG CONTENTED" all
right: "FOR HE CANNOT TAKE AWAY OUR JAZZ"
"AND WE CANNOT TAKE AWAY HIS TUNE." "IF HE
SAYS IT IS BAD" "WE SAY IT IS GOOD." "IF HE CALLS
US DEPRAVED" "WE CALL HIM RACIST" "THEN
THERE WAS A TIME WHEN THEY TOOK OUR
MUSIC AND PLAYED THEIR OWN INSTEAD OF
THE OLD ONE THAT WOULDN'T GO WITH THEIR
NEW LANGUAGE,"

etcetera:
"NOW IF THEY WANT TO DO THAT AGAIN LET THEM GO AHEAD AND DO IT ALL OVER AGAIN..."

But when they come back after their break from composing new songs for us-"they can find no one who sings them anymore but themselves alone..." "Then at last Negroes shall be free of this mighty lie."

"Well now...That was fun wasn't it? Now I want you both girls out there listening tonight because you heard two poets giving each other some good advice as well as great encouragement.... Let me give YOU some good advice, young lady. You should get yourself a typewriter and start writing poems in the old-fashioned way. Then you could make copies of them and send them to magazines...And I'll tell you this too: If they don't accept your work, just keep sending it out until they do! And if it takes ten years for that to happen, well then so be it! It's worth waiting for....So keep on keeping on with what you're doing...Keep composing those poems..."

"I want each one of you listening tonight to take home some good advice from these two girls here who are both poets themselves..."

"Well now...Goodnight everybody!"

II. WARPLAND 2.0 [11]

This poem has been banned because of the word "jazz"

>>> in it. I read it in Russia, and they understood me perfectly; so much so that they wanted me to write another poem about jazz, which I did. But here, many people are offended by the word "jazz."

They think I'm writing about black people. Well, I am. But it's not only about black people. It's about everybody who is alive and enjoys music. And I'm always surprised that there should be any question about a poem of mine being banned because of something like this. It's just part of life. And I don't know why they don't understand that. I suppose they think I'm writing propaganda for the NAACP or something like that.

But this poem was written back in the thirties when these things were not supposed to happen, but they did happen, and have been happening ever since then. It was not written to be political at all, but just to be a part of life. And it is a part of life. That's why it's here today in a book written by a woman whose name is Gwendolyn Brooks. And she's written many books for children as well as for adults, and she has always been interested in the life of the people around her, and she has always been

---

[11] GPT3 Warpland 2.0 | temp .55 | frequency and presence penalties .25

interested in getting her work into their hands and hearts and minds, if possible. And she knows how much poetry does for us all. So you see how wrong it is for anyone to try to ban a Gwendolyn Brooks poem!—especially when it's by Gwendolyn Brooks herself!—and she's got plenty more in her head and on her paper, too!—and she'll keep on giving us more and more if we'll just let her do it!—and we should let her do it!—and we should enjoy what she gives us because she knows what we need to know and she wants to give it to us!—and we should take advantage of the fact that we can get a great deal of good stuff right at our doorsteps if we just reach out our hands and take it!—because it's there!—for us!" —Gwendolyn Brooks: "Here is my poem 'Jazz.'"

"JAZZ"

This is jazz: / this is what jazz is: / this is jazz: / this is what jazz means: / this is jazz: / this is what jazz means: / this is jazz: / this is what jazz means: / this is jazz: / this is what jazz means: / this is jazz: / this is what jazz means: / this is jazz: / this is what jazz means: / this is jazz: / This is jazz. This is jazz. This is jazz. This is jazz. This is jazz. This is jazz. This is jazz. This is jazz. This is jazz. This is jazz. This is jazz. This is jazz. This is jazz."

—"Jazz" (unpaged)
Reprinted by permission of Harper & Row, Publishers, Inc., New York, New York

III. WARPLAND 2.0 [12]

This poem has been banned because of the word "jazz"

>>> in it. I tell them is to watch the movie "The Cotton Club" where this very music is being played. and you see the dancers. That's a different kind of dancing than what they're used to seeing on television. They know that, but they refuse to believe that it was really happening, even in the 1920s and 30s up until the 1950s when many of these musicians were still alive and working. It's interesting how people like to believe that African-Americans did not have any fun at all before the 1960s. But we had fun and this poem is a testimony to some of our fun and excitement. And we're still having fun. I've been saying that this poem is so current that it could have been written yesterday instead of nearly forty years ago.... And I'm going to leave it at that.

The word jazz itself can be a little trouble sparks because people who don't understand about its origins feel that it should be banned for obvious reasons. But I'll tell you just what I told them in my workshop... After all jazz is based on music which, as we all know, begins in heaven. We hear it and we're inspired, so there must be something good about it—otherwise God wouldn't have created it!

---

[12] GPT3 Warpland 2.0 | temp .75 | frequency and presence penalties .25

I'll tell you what else happened in this poem: When the speaker mentions "the perfume from burning pine," she isn't talking about Christmas trees. She's talking about lynching trees. So much has been missed from this poem!

IV. WARPLAND 2.0 [13]

This poem has been banned because of the word "jazz"

>>> in the first line. I have heard that it is impossible to teach this poem in any high school in Tulsa. It might be mentioned that no library normally has a copy of A Street in Bronzeville. You must go specially to find one in Tulsa, for instance. But you will be told that it is not on their shelves because of irrelevance and non-whiteness. So much for Tulsa! Imagine trying to imagine what can happen elsewhere! I think from now on, every time I say/envision/assume "Oklahoma," should automatically get "Tulsa" plastered against all possible references!"

Anyway, about my poem...well...you all know about your Oklahoma Public Library Service. And here, during late Winter and early Spring, the little seeds just seem to let the songs have already begun growing into fine fruit! My book was purchased by many libraries....for themselves and also as gifts toward love promotions at churches and schools and work places. Besides this there is the free distribution service explained by Lee Stone's magic comment: 'By giving books to people who wouldn't necessarily buy them, we are perpetuating a race of readers." Does that kind of give you more light? That's official League Trivia 101 explanations." Do you like the sound

---

[13] GPT3 Warpland 2.0 | temp 1.0 | frequency and presence penalties .50

of Official Action?" How successfully THAT title speaks! Translation: The League is organized enough to indulge some expenditures put forth under official titles for poetic or creative effectuators. Translation again: You may read poems (or hear them recited) at public gatherings; you may conduct workshops open even -are especially OPEN--to non-participants capable Of furnishing sandwiches!!! We want crowds!!! Have fun!!! Run around!! Under our supervision!! Who needs scholastics? Can you imagine yourself using that word with us?????? Has writing ever been so exciting? Who needs WITs? We need FEELings!! And conviviality all around!!!!!! Yes indeedy, Official Action makes things happen!

V. WARPLAND 2.0 [14]

This poem has been banned because of the word "jazz"

>>>in it. I wanted to say "this is what they're feeling. They're really true to themselves. They really love jazz." And so sometimes it's banned because of the word "jazz." Other times it's banned because of the words "lily white" in the first stanza, and certain black people think lily whiteness is something that you should never speak about—that you just have to reject such a condition with all your might. But as far as I'm concerned, lily whiteness could be a state of being that some black people would like to be in at various times, either for survival or for comfort and that's quite understandable. Anyway, this poem has been banned from anthologies and classes and so on, mostly because of these two words. Nobody wants to deal with them at all, neither of them: not jazz nor lily white!

---

[14] GPT3 Warpland 2.0 | temp .84 | frequency and presence penalties .50

TELL ME A BLACK STORY

I. GPT3

tell me a Black story

>>>A young black girl is walking home from school one day when she notices a group of white boys following her. She quickened her pace, but they began to run after her. She starts to run, but they catch up to her and knock her to the ground. They begin to kick her and call her names. She covers her head and curls into a ball, trying to protect herself. Suddenly, she feels someone pulling her away and she opens her eyes to see a black man standing over her, shielding her from the boys. He tells them to leave her along and they run off. The man helps the girl to her feet and walks her home, making sure she gets there safely.

II. WARPLAND 2.0

tell me a Black story

>>>And I'll tell them stories I've heard. I'll read them poetry. I read to them a great deal of Langston Hughes's poetry, and I read them some of my own work. I want to make them as literary as possible. I try to help them love books. I don't want to make them bookworms, but I do want them to love books. I want them to know that there are books out there that concern them, that have been written by them and about them. I want them to have that understanding. I try to stress the importance of reading. And I do this over and over again. I'm not a teacher, but I do my best. I talk to them. I laugh with them. I cry with them. I listen to them.

III. GPT3

tell me a Black story

>>>Once upon a time, there was a Black family who lived in a small town in the middle of nowhere. They were the only Black family in the town and they were always the last to get everything. The kids always had to sit in the back of the bus, the family always had to eat at the back of the restaurant, and they always had to live in the worst part of town. One day, the family decided they'd had enough. They packed up their things and moved to a big city where they could be around other Black people and be treated better. They never looked back.

IV. WARPLAND 2.0

tell me a Black story

>>>and I will tell them a story about Blacks. I know them very well, and I'm not afraid to say what I feel. I know that some of them are not going to like what I have to say. But I also know that some of them will like what I have to say. I can't imagine how they can't. I tell them that they are beautiful. I tell them that they are wonderful, and that they can go on the stage, and they can go into the movies, and they can get very rich and they can get immortal. And they can do all these things if they just work hard and are not afraid. I tell them that some of them will be so great that they will be a part of the language, and that people will say, "What does Auden mean when he says so and so?" And people will say, "Why, he means exactly what So-and-So meant." I tell them that they can be recognized and that they can be loved by everyone. I tell them that I love them and that I respect them and that I admire their beautiful faces and their beautiful bodies. I tell them that I am so happy that they are here.

V. GPT3 [15]

tell me a Black story

>>>Once upon a time, there was a black family who lived in the inner city. They were very poor and struggled to make ends meet. However, they were a close-knit family and loved each other dearly. One day, the father was killed in a drive-by shooting. The family was devastated. However, they pulled together and leaned on each other for support. They eventually overcame their grief and went on to lead happy and successful lives.

[15] GPT3 Davinci | temp .5 | frequency and presence penalties .5

VI. WARPLAND 2.0 [16]

tell me a Black story

>>> I realize that there are Black stories that have not been told. I want to tell them.

I am not a poet like Gwendolyn Brooks, but I am a poet, and I feel that these stories are worth telling. And I will tell them. I want to tell them. And I am going to keep writing poetry until the day I die. I don't know if it's any good or not, but I'm going to keep on doing it. It seems to be a natural thing for me to do. And I want to keep on doing it. And when the time comes that I can't do it anymore, then I'll be dead and buried with my poetry in my hand. But even then, the poetry will still be there for those who are interested in it. Poetry is something that will always be there for whoever is interested in it. And that's why I'm sure that people will still read my poetry long after I'm gone.

You know, we talk about how few Blacks are published today, and how few Blacks were published several years ago—and how few Blacks will be published in the future. But you know, people have always said such things when there were only a few Black writers around—when there were only a few Black writers publishing their work in this country and in the world.

---

[16] GPT3 Warpland 2.0 | temp .5 | frequency and presence penalties .5

And look at all the wonderful people who have been published! Look at all of the wonderful people who have been published during this time when we've been talking about how very few Black writers are publishing their work! So if we're going to look at this as a positive thing—if we're going to look at this as an opportunity for us to go out and publish our work—then why not take advantage of this situation? Why not go out and publish our work? Why not write our stories? Why not write our poetry? Why not write our essays? Why not paint our paintings? If you're a painter, why not paint your paintings? If you're a sculptor, why not sculpt your sculptures? If you're a dancer, why not dance your dances? If you're an actor, why not act your roles? If you're a musician, why not play your music? If you're a singer, why not sing your songs? Go out and do all of these things. And if you can't get published right away, keep on trying.

VII. GPT3 [17]

tell me a Black story

>>>A Black story is a story about the African American experience. It can be historical, contemporary, or personal.

[17] GPT3 Davinci | temp .75 | frequency and presence penalties .25

VIII. WARPLAND 2.0 [18]

tell me a Black story

>>>Tell me a story in which Negroes are kind to each other, and not only mean, but really interested in each other's welfare.

I am not trying to be funny. I believe that is true.

I do believe that if you are a reporter and have any respect for yourself—you must find some of these stories and record them. It is happening all over the country. I guess you know that. And if you want to, add your personal sympathy and help to black people in trouble, wherever it is you find them. You can contribute much to the cause of brotherhood by writing sympathetically about blacks who are struggling for a piece of the pie.

If you want to make your reports really effective, get out of the city if you have to and go where the fight is really being fought. Don't sit in the city and phone your dispatch back to your city desk: go there! And report! Take pictures! Film them for all you're worth. Make sure that what you've recorded can be heard or seen by your audience back home.

---

[18] GPT3 Davinci | temp .75 | frequency and presence penalties .25

When I was young, I knew black reporters who would go out of their way not only to hear but even to record what was happening on a hot street corner in Cicero or Cicero-land. The fight between blacks and whites is not going to go on forever, but while it does last, we have a chance now (because we didn't have it when segregation was legal) to record exactly what is happening. We have our chance right now to record what happens in Mississippi at night—something we could never do when segregation was the law. But now there are always white reporters around. And I think it is important for us always to remember that this is our chance, our golden opportunity, to help our people while they are continuing their struggle! Please use this opportunity with full enthusiasm! Use this opportunity with full import! Report on everything you can see! Report on everything you can hear! Report on everything you can feel!

IX. GPT3 [19]

tell me a Black story

>>>In the early 1800s, a young Black girl is born into slavery in the American South. She works hard every day, laboring in the fields or in the house, never knowing when she will be sold away from her family. One day, she is brought to the auction block and purchased by a kind-hearted woman who teaches her to read and write. The girl eventually learns of the Underground Railroad and decides to risk everything for a chance at freedom. She makes her way north, dodging slave catchers along the way, until she finally reaches safety in Canada.

[19] GPT3 Davinci | temp .75 | frequency and presence penalties .5

X. WARPLAND 2.0 [20]

tell me a Black story

>>>and it seems to them a fresh vow.
When they have just heard Paul Laurence Dunbar recite "We Wear the Mask." An interesting thing happened as a result of that poem. A number of young Blacks said they had always been told that they didn't understand poetry and couldn't appreciate it, so they used this piece as an excuse not to read poetry. Well, we want them to read it. We want them to read anything that challenges their intellects and excites their emotions into wanting more from the world around them.
So I'm going to make a special point of emphasizing how absolutely wonderful Black poets are. I'm going to quote many of their poems for them (and for whites too) so that there is no excuse for anyone who would be interested in poetry not being able to find some poet whose work touches him or her deeply.
In addition, I hope soon to publish an anthology—I hope it will be published by September—that will include many of our best writers including Langston Hughes, Sterling Brown, Countee Cullen, Albert Murray...you name the names you wish, there are many excellent ones—Jabari Njoroge Njego....
There should be plenty here for all tastes so that this might provide a bridge between main-stream poetry and our own

---

[20] GPT3 Davinci | temp .85 | frequency and presence penalties .5

Black poets' poetry. There isn't too much emphasis on studying literature these days and less attention paid than ever before perhaps since the Renaissance brought forth its Giants such as Chaucer and Shakespeare.... We're lowering standards everywhere except in sports...well...let's not speak about sports either.... But certainly we can expect our school boards at any level at least to fulfill their responsibility in providing some basic books for study in secondary schools....

But then again nobody expects much anymore of White people, do we? They'll come along with their good intentions toward us but always toward themselves first all the time!... When whites said "Thurgood Marshall," what did they first think? How could Justice Thurgood Marshall help white people more than blacks? So everybody hopes he'll win his case quickly because if he does white folks can go home feeling good about themselves again! On game day you see lots of little children going about with Jesse Jackson buttons on their shirts or jackets...but when have you seen oh say...running down the street...a Poet Laureate's button?

XI. GPT3 [21]

tell me a Black story

>>>Black Panther-The story of T'Challa, heir to the hidden but advanced kingdom of Wakanda, who must step forward to lead his people into a new era and must confront a challenger from his country's past.

---

[21] GPT3 Davinci | temp .7 | frequency and presence penalties 0

XII. WARPLAND 2.0 [22]

tell me a Black story

>>>
if they know one, tell me a Black story,
if they know one. Tell me
about the Black enigma,
tell me about the Black reality.
Tell me about the Black conundrum.
Tell me about the Black en-
thrallment. Tell me about the
Black enchantment. Tell me
about the Black
Bewitchment. Tell me
about the Black
Bewilderment. Tell me
about the Black
Bewil-
derment. Tell me about the Black
Bewilderment. Tell me about
the Black
Effulgence. Tell me about the Black
Effulgence. Tell me about the Black
Enigma. Tell me about the Black

---

[22] GPT3 Warpland 2.0 | temp .7 | frequency and presence penalties 0

Enigma. Tell me about the Black
Enthrallment. Tell me about the Black
Enthrallment. Tell me about the Black
Enthusiasm. Tell me about the Black
Enthusiasm. Tell me

ONCE UPON A TIME, MAUD MARTHA

once upon a time, Maud Martha went [23]

>>>to a party. I have to tell you about the party, because it is part of the story. The story is about Maud Martha's going to a party and meeting a man who is not her boyfriend, and this man kisses her, and she kisses him back, and she goes home with him. And that's all there is to the story, although I have written a poem about it, which I will give you later.

But the party is an important part of the story. That's why I want to describe it for you. It was a very large party in a very big house on the South Side of Chicago. This was in the days when people lived on the South Side of Chicago. There were many rooms in this house, many rooms on many floors. And there were many lights and many people. And there were many drinks and many smokes. And there was music playing in the background, so you couldn't hear what anybody else was saying. And there were many mirrors all around so that you could see yourself over and over again. And there were mirrors even in the bathroom on the first floor so you could see yourself even when you went to urinate or to defecate or whatever you call it.

I think that's enough description of that party for now. But I'll

---

[23] GPT3 Warpland 2.0 | temp .55 | frequency and presence penalties .25

tell you more about parties later on, if you would like me to do that for you.

Now we come to other things that happened to Maud Martha before she went to this party. And after she came from this party. In fact a lot happened before she got there and after she left. She met people at parties before she got married and after she got married; but we're not going to talk about those parties just now. We're going to talk about these parties that happened before she met her man at this party we've described so far; and then what happened after she met him at this party we've described so far.

So let's go back to the beginning of Maud Martha's life, which we haven't mentioned yet-and maybe won't mention now either-but which begins with her being born in Chicago, Illinois, on a certain date which has no importance whatsoever in this story except that it was in 1923, or perhaps 1924-I'm not sure which-and I'll tell you why later on if I can remember why it doesn't matter when she was born at all.

once upon a time, Maud Martha went [24]

>>>to a party. It was at a penthouse.

Last to arrive, she ran up five flights of iron-shaking stairs to ring a bell in a semi-vacant room where lights were off and everyone was dancing. It did not occur to her that she might wait below, whereat direct stairway mercy might be had.

Nor did it occur to the boy who came panting after her after she had rung the bell. He was thin but strong enough by any test to get a well-nourished grip on the fruit of her until then undistressed shoulder, and suddenly whirl her so as to evanesce futilely against wall-to-wall terrace life. In point of fact, at that time and place it was impossible for her not to dance, given her exciting heritage (she knew nothing else) and especially when placed visibly before wall-to-wall excited anything that wiggled. And some of them did wiggle outrageously.

She accepted this dance because he seemed so eager; and because (though it worried her not at all) there might be an end product similar to what was accepted among her Gentile friends. She knew that often you were kissed at parties, in alleys or closeupon cars, you called them. She didn't call them anything. She secretly looked forward to exciting kissing, if it

---

[24] GPT3 Warpland 2.0 | temp 1.0 | frequency and presence penalties .25

came along just right—though if for some reason she were bald let alone alien, that would cancel all thought of kissing; also had already canceled that deprivation, as soon as possible, forever, because why should such horror come! To cancel such horror forever though, she still ached, especially at movies when a man took a woman in his arms...

Her weak strength drained out rapidly through happy heels and around encircling elbow; and the next thing she could remember beyond grinning abasement would be clinging wall which was good but lacked useful traction below.

She fancied herself alone in a certain kind of room at night; and it was dark so that more advanced enjoyment might come forth than on beautiful thick rich lightboned lifebeaming terrace. She would have been nurtured by these people till she didn't know what [was] happening. Underwater speech occurred and meanwhile tapping toes clicked everlastingly against resolute floor. Then something like wine came bubbling up armsbodytobeam and underneath the thin cloth (or silk or nylon whatever was the party wear) there were some things like bugs running.

Once upon a time Maud Martha went[25]

>>>to the theater. She found a seat, felt the velvet of her plush tickle her thighs. She was unperturbed--in fact, did she not deserve velvet? The lights went out, and a unity in darkness hovered over 1200 people. She waited for what was to come--the deft shifting of darkness into light, into another unity, this time one that would speak and sing rather than impress in ponderous silence. A hush arose over a thousand people. They were quiet while they watched the ceremony called "Overture."

She did not hate the word, but wondered what a proper approximation would be.... Then came the Ringing In (important too), at which the voices of instruments mingled with human voices.... The acts of the play were performed in a serene exclusiveness that smiled upon her. The curtain like some final formality falling; quite as if she were surrounded by suave cavaliers. ... One or two scenes led her to be glad again that men had not excluded them from Shakespeare's stage. Glorious poems crept almost to her fingertips and stayed there, never quite coming to rest... Wise prologues touched her intelligence like the finger-tips of an old friend.... Now and then affronts came, but these either soon went away or became blithely welcome when their spirits got hold of her... She was gratified. Everything was just as it should be...she felt

---

[25] GPT3 Warpland 2.0 | temp 1.0 | frequency and presence penalties .25

it instantly...Her spinal cord relaxed, registered this truth and took a little nap...

She slept wanting realities to ensue in which she should figure as one who knew how things would always be.... And so it is that when Maud Martha worked up a lather over some vicious hope killed, she remembered those nights of remembered peace.... (She felt how good life might be.)... For then she saw how one particular killing could prove the world right, could prove it rich in imagination and rich in beneficence toward those who had their eyes set on things that should die: flowers, say; or turtles; or babies...Hadn't nothing natural ever died?... All must come to an end…

The essence of death is mere relative end-stuff—it does not matter enough not to come back.... And so it was necessary for this particular plant to plow under...Something else would rise...

Once upon a time Maud Martha went

>>>to a party. It was a costume party. Maud Martha went as a queen.

She wore her mother's old velvet coat with its fur collar, a farthingale and a veil . . . her sister left the old velvet coat at home, went to the party without it . . . and got pneumonia. Maud Martha decided not to go out of doors at all for a long time.

She sat by the windows in her house and dreamed of a way that she might always know when it was nice weather, either too cold or too hot, so she could do nothing on such days as these except sit by the windows and wonder how she might be told when it was safe to go out.

Her mother used to tell her to watch the barber-shop sign across the street because when she saw snow it would be advisable to cover herself well with wraps; when she saw sun it would be good enough. But she never saw snow or sun because the barber shop was closed down before there was any chance of looking out of her window and seeing these things. So she stayed indoors, and waited for the barber shop to reopen… Then she saw neither snow nor sun for the barber shop

---

[26] GPT3 Warpland 2.0 | temp .85 | frequency and presence penalties .25

continued to hang its "Closed" sign in spite of temperatures rising or falling as high or low as they might be expected to go in Southside Chicago.

When finally the barber shop opened again, Maud Martha went out and got pneumonia...

Now Maud Martha could not afford an overcoat or any other outer wrap at that time. Yet, if she had had an overcoat like her sister's... Her mother later bought her a new velvet coat with no fur collar and no farthingale.... but without an overcoat like her sister's... Maud Martha decided that she would never again venture beyond doors without such protection as an overcoat affords. So Maud Martha gave up ever going outside again...and spent many hours staring blankly into looking-glasses trying to see what life Outside looked like.

Then one night just before bedtime Maud Martha's mother came home from some sort of illiciting endeavor and announced that Maud Martha would be going out of doors within a very few minutes...to go sailing down Southside streets in the family automobile.... (They were rich, then) and there were two surprises awaiting her.

One was that they were going to drive around Southside streets but only during daytime hours and only during summertime months . . . (Southside streets in the family automobile!) and second, that she was going to be given an overcoat... Then

Maud Martha knew that she could leave her curtains alone and gaze out of them whenever the spirit moved.... She put on the overcoat...and rode in the car....and was given a lot of money.

And Maud Martha thought it a wonderful idea to give money to people she met along Southside streets...so she gave some to several. But, as usual, they did nothing but stare at her. In her excitement, Maud Martha noticed nothing amiss, until she noticed that the two were not giving anything back. She told them so... but neither seemed aware that this was customary in ordinary "street" transactions... Even her father had never noticed this before when he bought her things. So Maud Martha stopped throwing money.

But there was yet another surprise awaiting her. There were many young people out on the streets and a great many of them wore their hair in ways previously unknown to Maud Martha. One boy said "How you're looking?"..."I'm looking" said Maud Martha... "Like what?" asked the boy..."Like this" said Maud Martha...."just like this." So the boy washed his hair and it came out looking exactly like hers. Another boy said "You're looking." "Like what?" asked Maud Martha...."like this," said he...and he washed his hair and it came out looking exactly like hers. Another boy said "You're looking." And asked her how she did it showed her how and it came out looking just like hers. And another boy said "How you do it" and showed how and it came out looking just like hers...and another one said "How you do it "and showed how and it came out looking just like hers...yet another one said "How you do it" showed how and it came out looking just like hers.

But when Maud Martha attempted to show them how to make hair just like hers ...they couldn't do it. There seemed almost no difference between their attempts and those of countless other persons who used to pass her house on the way to school outside...except that those failed persons used not to stop at her windows for comparison purposes but continued walking on by.... Without ever stopping to compare notes with themselves or with each other...just passing on by... It's very strange, thought Maud Martha...going once more beyond doors . . .

Once upon a time, Maud Martha went [27]

>>>to a party in Firestone Terrace, and met a handsome duke. It was the last time she would have kind looks. The duke did not find it worth his time to go on with her, because she was not the lovely lady that the lovely lady next to her was. He then gave his attention only to the gorgeous lady. She was more gratifying than Maud Martha who had never been so much as to any place before because Maud Martha did not have a car. No white man had ever asked her out before then or since then, or had never come up to her on the street and told her that she was the prettiest girl he'd ever seen or asked her out on a date. And now you know why white men don't come up to you on the street and ask you out on dates. Because they are just prejudiced that way. And they like women who cook them free meals.

No they don't like anybody else to give them a free meal. If they married black women they would want to do their own cooking even if they married movie actresses like scandalous Lena Horne. They want these women to cook for them and look after their children and everything. But now Maud Martha sat by herself in Firestone Terrace. And she wrote poetry all night long, through white noise, through sips of lemonade, through dances with white boys too young for love making, through "rolls"--twenty-five boys in succession--through talk about

---

[27] GPT3 Warpland 2.0 | temp .9 | frequency and presence penalties .25

clothes and make up and faces and men... until at last came a knock at her door, upon which was written "Maud Martha."

An invitation to heaven's doorstep? No; it was an invitation for her to join the gang of "bounders," as our Negroes say, who were going in an empty pick-up truck around behind a schoolhouse... And there was Simalee, whom Maud Martha vaguely knew from a tiny corner store where poor Maud bought such small necessities as pantyhose and cigarettes.

"Are you going with those guys in that empty truck?" Told yes, Maud received instructions: "Sit right up front next to Eddie and hold his hand when you get scared." So off went this group of riders through woods behind schools, into canals by fire places through all manner of exploring adventures while certainly some two dozen automobiles were bumping over bumps through the streets of Cicero, Fox Lake, Barrington Hills...

Two dread lines for what, Maud wondered? Two double-frowned lines, on a hot dusty summer night demanded by white people: a show of passing respect to their false but dominant specialness. Aha! Even whites who owned nothing wanted at least that much, too. And so they displayed themselves. Ah, what a display they made of their viciousness, too. A new and awful day in the annals of ugliness and raw showing-off.

Maud rode thus with companions down, west, north and east

into all kinds of strange adventure; squares, crescents streets (during which past persons begged her not to go down--but why not), avenues large and malls small.... Down one lane she remarked three policemen in an alleyway leaving a recent beatism after they had beaten down some new chap in Cicero doings...

Across from a store was a young girl washing her face; she knew what that was for. Belts and long beards, long mustaches... all these must be clean for the elders sat at home to watch the proceedings. Two boys a block or so away were playing with firecrackers... The blasts had grown to resounding volumes near Maud's ears by the time she got home. Just in time to get strength up...

Enough white folks were happy with what they had just seen, enough white folks felt cheerful at last...So they had themselves a whistle now after the whistle they had called out earlier and before the whistle still before...Yes there was great jubilation among the urgers toward closing time...And there was great jubilation among them when it actually came...Then there was a great white holiday for one night at least...They got their TV home again...They put their kids to bed and enjoyed themselves.

There was Some Movie Playing At The Campus Tonight. Yes yes yes. She didn't know whether it was one she'd ever seen or not. She supposed it was one she'd never seen, because if it was one she'd seen she would certainly have noticed something about it... But this wasn't important anyway.... What was important was that little Annie and Willy would go To Sleep After An Hour or so of sweet cooling compresses applied by Mother and Father, Jr., ...and there were refreshers and cold lemonades in the kitchen refrigerator, heavy with fruit juice stands on shelves... pale reds and blues and greens inside compact spring-doors....

Maud stood under a ricer and pressed her arms for five minutes. And she thought of white people, who liked to lie down flat under straight whistles and machines, to be relieved of their ailments. She thought of white people who liked to be pumped, too, having appetite for that operation alone, not for its result. Neither did white people care for absoluteness. They would like to pump their peck- leys; they would like to reduce their dislikes...They liked themselves rounder, softer, ever more comprehensive...They didn't want any dents in their persons.

Maud Martha received an angry telephone call.... Oh she was not so good! Why did she give herself such airs? What right had she to stray around with that gang? What right had she to play with firecrackers? What right had she to be out so late at night with those fellows? That was no life for a young girl!... Why did she hold her head high so much? Why did she waste her time listening at the radio after ten o'clock when she knew she should be studying...studying...Oh she had too many tricks up her sleeve!... "Lousy female!" Full menacing range of tone:

"Whore!"... The phone went dead...

Maud had felt good before the call, but now what good was there? It hurt a little...And another one: "Sister! I hear you're out every night." "I heard about it." "You shouldn't let yourself be seen with them kinds."... "Women of our race are not like that." "But this is what I've always been told," said Maud patiently. "You surely don't want it all to stop?" demanded Maud. "Well it should have stopped then." "Then what will I do?" Maud's choice facing a wide air was only one: either run or stand. She stood alertly adjusting her hands in pockets...Then came another voice from Africa apparently: "If you keep going on the way you're going, girlie, you'll be the devil's bed warmer before too long!" Maud must choose again between running or standing more firmly than ever... but now with more anger starting to fight in her heart for a slice of freedom.

And Maud chose to stand firmest because now there was anger in her heart. How dare he say such a thing! How dare he!

Once upon a time, Maud Martha went [28]

>>>to the alley and killed a rat. She killed it quickly. She felt no pang. She felt nothing. She did not hate the creature. She did not go to the creature's home and cry over broken possessions. She simply killed it and went on about her business. She may have enjoyed the smell of the blood then, and looked at its innards with a certain attention, but she felt no regrets about what she had done.

When Maud Martha did this, she was extremely clear and comparatively cool. But later on, when Maud Martha was feeling sick, sick, sick, she tore her hair, she stuttered; she fainted; she felt physical pain in her stomach; she wondered if now, if ever, she could join another "Round Robin" again; she wondered how long would she be ashamed; how long would that crawly feeling be in her stomach; how long would the thing disgust her; how long would her neighbors look at her with uneasy eyes; how long would they say among themselves that still another Black has gone crazy...

Later on, when Maud Martha had become aware of being homesick for Chicago, for Philadelphia, for Pittsburgh, she wanted so badly, wanted so much to be there again in those darkly-rowdy cities...she stood upon her height in those cities,

---

[28] GPT3 Warpland 2.0 | temp .9 | frequency and presence penalties .25

and people applauded. And here in Yonkers...in Yonkers... there was no applause; only that quiet look which told…told... what was it? Was it "Get back," or "Who are you?" Or was it something else? What was that look....which told.... Yes , later on when Maud Martha got sick enough to be better again, later on when Maud Martha thought of joining another "Round Robin," later on when Maud Martha decided that any more nights like this one should find her playing Bop instead of Bach on the phonograph...Why!...Maud Martha might soon find herself canvassing this street buying Coca Colas for everybody in sight. Yes!...Maud Martha might next time perhaps want all of these folks to sit down with their Coca Cola cans at a big silver table filled with beefsteak and greens. Yes!...Maud Martha might want everyone to talk together. Maud Mary-Almost certainly Maud Mary-might want everyone to get along together…to get right together...and then...then maybe...even perhaps.....Yes! Perhaps even then, perhaps even then…

ACKNOWLEDGMENTS

This work is indebted to the writing of Gwendolyn Brooks.

LILLIAN-YVONNE BERTRAM is an African American writer, poet, artist, and educator who works at the intersection of computation, AI, race, and gender. They are the author of *Travesty Generator* (Noemi Press), a book of computational poetry that received the Poetry Society of America's 2020 Anna Rabinowitz prize for interdisciplinary work and was longlisted for the 2020 National Book Award for Poetry. They are the recipient of a National Endowment for the Arts Poetry Fellowship. Their other poetry books include *How Narrow My Escapes* (*DIAGRAM*/New Michigan), *Personal Science* (Tupelo Press), *a slice from the cake made of air* (Red Hen Press), and *But a Storm is Blowing From Paradise* (Red Hen Press). Their most recent book, *Negative Money*, was published in 2023.

☼

COLOPHON

Text is set in a digital version of Jenson, designed by Robert Slimbach in 1996, and based on the work of punchcutter, printer, and publisher Nicolas Jenson. The titles here are in Futura, which is the best font for titles.

✲

NEW MICHIGAN PRESS, based in Tucson, Arizona, prints poetry and prose chapbooks, especially work that transcends traditional genre. Together with *DIAGRAM*, NMP sponsors a yearly chapbook competition.

DIAGRAM, a journal of text, art, and schematic, is published bimonthly at THEDIAGRAM.COM. Periodic print anthologies are available from the New Michigan Press at NEWMICHIGANPRESS.COM.

www.ingramcontent.com/pod-product-compliance
Lightning Source LLC
LaVergne TN
LVHW052356100826
845147LV00013B/854

* 9 7 8 1 9 3 4 8 3 2 9 3 6 *